George Lewis Prentiss, Assoc. of the Alumni of Bowdoin College

The Free Christian State and the Present Struggle

an address delivered before the Association of the alumni of Bowdoin

college - Vol. 1

George Lewis Prentiss, Assoc. of the Alumni of Bowdoin College

The Free Christian State and the Present Struggle
an address delivered before the Association of the alumni of Bowdoin college - Vol. 1

ISBN/EAN: 9783337264277

Printed in Europe, USA, Canada, Australia, Japan

Cover: Foto ©Lupo / pixelio.de

More available books at **www.hansebooks.com**

The Free Christian State and the Present Struggle.

AN ADDRESS

DELIVERED BEFORE THE

ASSOCIATION

OF THE

ALUMNI OF BOWDOIN COLLEGE.

BY

GEORGE L. PRENTISS,

AUGUST 8, 1861.

New-York :

PUBLISHED BY W. H. BIDWELL,

AT THE OFFICE OF THE AMERICAN THEOLOGICAL REVIEW,

No. 5 Beekman Street.

1861.

Bowdoin College, August 8th, 1861.

Rev. Geo. L. Prentiss, D.D. :

Dear Sir : At the close of the Address delivered by you this day, before the Association of the Alumni of Bowdoin College, it was voted unanimously, the audience rising in concurrence, "That the thanks of the Association be presented to the Rev. Dr. Prentiss, for his refreshing and eloquent Address on the Free Christian State, and a copy be requested for the press."

In behalf of the Alumni Association,

EGBERT C. SMYTH, *Secretary.*

———•••———

Newport, August 13th, 1861.

My Dear Sir : I cheerfully comply with the request of the Association of the Alumni, and hereby place the Address at their disposal.

Yours, most truly,

GEO. L. PRENTISS.

Prof. E. C. Smyth, *Secretary.*

ADDRESS.

—•••—

Mr. President and Brethren of the Alumni :

It has been customary, on occasions like the present, to discuss some topic of general literary interest, or as was so happily done at your meeting three years ago,* to revive the pleasant memories and rehearse the honors of our *Alma Mater*. But I shall offer no apology for departing from this custom to-day. The stern realities of the hour suggest a subject coming home more directly to our business and bosoms. Heretofore we have met to look each other in the face and take sweet counsel together as old friends and sons of Bowdoin : to-day we meet rather as fellow-citizens and common children of the imperilled republic ; and it is our country which claims our first and chief thought.

Without further preface, then, allow me to speak to you of the Free Christian State, as developed in the history and institutions of our Union, and of the dangers which beset it.† A free state is the grandest phenomenon of civilization. It is one of the rarest also. Of the

---

* In an address by Professor Packard, entitled, "Our Alma Mater."

† I here use the word state, of course, in the most comprehensive sense, and include in it the family, and the temporal institution of the Church also. In its spiritual character, as "the mystical body of Christ," the Church rises far above all earthly states, belongs to no country or age, and is identical with the everlasting kingdom of God.

host of governments which have risen and disappeared
in the course of time, only one here and there could be
called free. The same may be said of those now existing. Of the five great powers, for example, which rule
the Old World, nobody, certainly, would pretend that
more than one is, in the proper sense of the term, a free
country. Certain forms and degrees of liberty exist,
no doubt, in the other four, especially in France and
Prussia. But in England alone is liberty fairly domesti-
cated, guarded by law and incorporated with the whole
life of the nation; in England alone is liberty a great
popular institution and chartered right. And still it
can not be denied that even in England we have but an
imperfect specimen of civil liberty. The idea of a free,
Christian state has never yet been absolutely realized,
nor dare we expect it ever will be until that blessed
consummation, predicted and longed for by saint and
sage, when the reign of Divine Justice shall have been
fully established on earth. In speaking of our own
country, then, I shall be far enough from assuming that
it is the ideal of a free or a Christian state. If it were,
we should not be engaged in mortal struggle for its existence. In order to appreciate and enjoy our inestimable
civil blessings, we need not claim a monopoly of them,
nor that we possess them as yet, in all their perfection.
This is no time to indulge in idle boasting and self-con-
ceit. Freedom is one of the old, tutelary divinities of
the race. We ought not to suppose that this is her
only or her last abode. Enough that she has always
loved to dwell here, and that here she inspired our
fathers to rear for her a temple more capacious than
was ever built before ; an ever-expanding Union of
well-ordered, constitutional government, which stretches
already across the continent.

I shall attempt no elaborate analysis of the nature of

the state and of its different forms. The scope of my argument does not require it. There are certain great principles which lie at the foundation of all true government, whatever its name. They are common to monarchy and to the republic. The reason and experience of mankind agree in declaring them to be immutable. They cannot be set at naught without involving society itself in ruins. They are written in such large and plain characters on the whole course of nature, that he who runs may read them. They are as old as man; yea, as the throne of God. Such essential organizing principles are law, order, justice, obedience and truth. Without these, government is only another name for anarchy or despotism. They are the adamantine pillars upon which repose all good things in earth and heaven. It is because the free Christian state is based upon and embodies such divine principles that we are entitled to call it the noblest phenomenon of civilization. In fact, it *is* civilization in visible strength, order and splendor. There is nothing else on earth so august or so puissant. It is the bright, consummate flower of a nation's life; "the Sabbath and port of all its labors and peregrinations." What varied powers conspire to form and enrich it! Nothing less than the intelligence, virtue, piety, industry, art, philosophy, learning and experience of the race. For, as it is the grandest, so also is it the slowest and most difficult growth of time. It is no exhalation of the morn, but ages are required to produce it. Ere it comes to its full birth, a people must have groaned and travailed together in pain for generations. It can no more be *improvised* than a personal character like Washington's, with all its wealth of ripened virtue and patriotism, can be formed in a day. How little the most thoughtful of us consider what a long and painful history lies back of every civil privilege we enjoy ! through what storms, and over what rough seas society has reached one port of safety after another !

In passing now to the special topic of this address, let me prepare the way by substituting for a moment in place of that somewhat formal term, the State, the more familiar term, Our Country. This is a household word, and intelligible alike to man, woman and child. It recalls at once the magnificent heritage of government, freedom, intelligence and religion, bequeathed to us by our venerated ancestors. These, in truth, make our country. They are its spiritual essence, its living soul. They clothe it with dignity and honor. They render it an object second only to the Divine Government itself in its claim upon our love and self-devotion. What is our country but another name for constitutional liberty, for authority founded in truth and uprightness, for the family and the church, in a word, for all the precious immunities and privileges of Christian society? Without these, it would be a mere geographical term, a name for so much area of land and water. But transfigured by these humanizing agencies, fashioned out of a rude mass of earth into stately forms of culture and civility, it rises far above all local description, and becomes the home and mighty rampart of our dearest rights and affections. It is a moral as well as physical entity ; and as such, can stretch forth its protecting arm to the ends of the earth. The starry emblem of its authority floats round the world. It is endowed with a kind of omnipresence ; for wherever beats the heart of a loyal American citizen, there is a pulsation of the nation's life. In this sense our country follows her children wherever they go. She attends the ministers of her will in royal and imperial courts. Whatever distant seas are ploughed by her ships of war, or of peaceful trade, her ægis is over them. She accompanies

our faithful missionaries as they go to plant the banner
of the cross upon the strongholds of pagan error and
superstition. She is, indeed, the strong protector, as
she is the benignant mother, of us all. Allegiance to
her is part of that religious fealty which we owe to the
eternal Sovereign of the universe. Such is our country:
the home and shrine of the sweetest charities and affections of our nature; the divinely appointed sphere of a
thousand weighty duties; the guardian and pledge of
our noblest temporal hopes and interests. Without it
we should be shelterless, home-sick wanderers on the
face of the earth; our social faculties, "rusting in us
unused," would bear naught but thorns and thistles,
instead of ripening into those generous public virtues
which are the fountain of so much happiness and honor
to the race; our high hopes for our children would
vanish into thin air, or rather, they would be changed
into gloomy fears and forebodings. Yes, robbed of our
country, of its government and laws, its freedom and
fair humanities, our condition would be as if

> "The cloud-capped towers, the gorgeous palaces,
> The solemn temples, the great globe itself;
> Yea, all which it inherit, should dissolve."

This great American system of liberty and social order, like our mother tongue, is a marvellous compo-
site of old and new. It is enriched by the spoils of
all time. Hardly any great state, ancient or modern,
but has contributed something to its generous and fair
proportions. What would it be if bereft of all it
owes to the legislation of Moses, and the Hebrew Scrip-
tures; to the democratic spirit, literature, and heroic
examples of Greece; or to the laws and jurisprudence of
republican and imperial Rome? It strikes its roots
deep into the mediaeval and early Christian ages. The

best politics of modern Europe helped to form it. The fountain from which it drew, and still draws, its holiest principles and inspiration, is the New Testament.

Never since the beginning of the world was a people allowed ampler scope, freely to avail itself of all the lights of history, and all the aids of reflection, in constructing a system of national polity; and never had a people a richer experience of its own, or a more invaluable body of existing laws and institutions wherewith to give harmony, strength, and perpetuity to the new structure. For, undoubtedly, the power which, above all others, inspired and shaped our republican system was the old Anglican liberty, which our fathers brought with them across the ocean. This, together with the institutions which have given it its marvellous vitality and strength in the mother country, such as municipal and local self-government, the town-meeting, the county court, popular suffrage and representation, the common law, the constable, trial by jury, the local church, the college, the Puritan Sabbath, and the old English Bible —this was and is the noblest substance of our national life. It is a mistake to suppose that our liberty is the fruit of the Revolutionary war. In that war we fought for and won our Independence; but our most important liberties are a venerable heir-loom of the Anglo-Saxon race. They were won for us at Runnymede, and on many a later field, renowned in the annals of British freedom. They were among those " true, ancient, and indubitable rights and liberties " of the people of England, asserted and claimed in their memorable Bill of Rights. Our Declaration of Independence was virtually a reässertion of these same " ancient rights and liberties." The Articles of Confederation were an attempt to combine and establish them in a " perpetual Union;" and finally the Constitution of the United

States organized them into our present system of national government. But, although the substance of our liberties was the most precious inheritance which the infant nation brought with it, I need not say how greatly they were increased and invigorated under the hardy discipline of the colonial period, and during the terrible trials of the war of Independence; or how, when the time was fully ripe, they were at length perfected in the great Constitution under which we now live. This Constitution was the work of men preëminent for public wisdom, zeal, prudence, and magnanimity; men deeply versed in the philosophy of government,

" Looking before and after——"

Long reflection, aided by much study and experience, had endowed them with a political sagacity almost intuitive; and in all this they only represented the enlightened popular instincts of the country. A more upright, single-hearted, admirable body of patriots never sat in council. They were worthy to be presided over by Washington.

"Great men were then among us; hands that penned
And tongues that uttered wisdom; better none.
.   .   .   .
They knew how genuine glory was put on;
Taught us how rightfully a nation shone
In splendor."

As we now look back and review their labors in the light of history, it seems little short of miraculous that they committed so few serious errors. The Constitution formed by these master-builders was intended, as has been intimated, to recapitulate and combine into one political system the substantial existing rights, liberties, and institutions of the country; adding what seemed needful and best fitted to crown the whole with

12

the unity, majesty, and force of national sovereignty. Such is the American Union. It took away from the several States little that had ever been theirs, except their weakness. It preserved and placed under better guaranties their local rights and authority. It *gave* them the freedom of the continent. This system has now been in operation nearly three quarters of a century, and its results are among the marvels of history. They have been the study of some of the deepest political thinkers and statesmen of modern times; and, I doubt not, Aristotle himself would have pondered them with wonder and delight. Never before was the spirit of democratic freedom and equality combined with the highest principles of law and authority in a manner so grand and effective.* Could the illustrious statesmen, who formed the Constitution, come back to earth, they would be lost in awe and amazement at the fruit of their own labors. Could the people of the United States, who ordained and established it, revisit the scenes so dear to them, they would fall upon their knees in adoration of that Almighty Providence which enabled them to transmit to their children such a matchless heritage. So it *would* have been a little while ago. *Now*, alas! their grateful wonder and adoration would be turned into speechless grief, as they saw a portion of their posterity scornfully trampling that goodly heritage under foot! For that *they* intended it should be

---

* The remarkable testimony of the Emperor of Russia, published since the delivery of this address, deserves to be here cited: "For the more than eighty years that it has existed, the American Union owes its independence, its towering rise, and its progress, to the concord of its members, consecrated, under the auspices of its illustrious founder, by institutions which have been able to reconcile the Union with liberty. This Union has been faithful. *It has exhibited to the world the spectacle of a prosperity without example in the annals of history.*"—*Prince Gortschakoff's Letter of July* 10.

perpetual, no candid student of American history can doubt for an instant. One might as reasonably doubt whether they expected the continent itself would be perpetual, or that their posterity would continue always to inhabit it. They had taken infinite pains to construct a permanent government; this had been, consciously or unconsciously, the aim of all their plans and toil; this was the ruling idea of the old Confederation. The articles constituting it were called "Articles of Perpetual Union;" and the last of them closes in this wise: "We do further solemnly plight and engage the faith of our respective constituents, . . that these Articles shall be inviolably observed by the States we respectively represent, and that the Union shall be perpetual." The experience of the Revolutionary war, and of the sad years immediately following, demonstrated that the Union thus formed was incapable of self-perpetuation. It was tainted with an incurable weakness. The famous Convention of 1787 was assembled to remedy this defect; and on the completion of their work it was adopted by the whole nation as its own, in this simple but truly august style:

"WE, THE PEOPLE OF THE UNITED STATES, IN ORDER TO FORM A MORE PERFECT UNION, ESTABLISH JUSTICE, INSURE DOMESTIC TRANQUILLITY, PROVIDE FOR THE COMMON DEFENCE, PROMOTE THE GENERAL WELFARE, AND SECURE THE BLESSINGS OF LIBERTY TO OURSELVES AND OUR POSTERITY, DO ORDAIN AND ESTABLISH THIS CONSTITUTION FOR THE UNITED STATES OF AMERICA."

He who can detect *secession* in this language, or in any of the articles which follow it, ought certainly to find no difficulty in proving from the Bible that there is no God! The Constitution, you perceive, did not pretend to *create* the Union, but only to render it more perfect. On this point it may be worth while to cite the very first sentences of the *Federalist*, written, as you know, by Hamilton, Madison and Jay, and addressed to the people of New-York : " After full experience of the insufficiency of the existing Federal Government, you are invited to deliberate upon a new Constitution for the United States of America. The subject speaks its own importance ; comprehending in its consequences nothing less than the existence [not the creation] of the Union ; the safety and welfare of the parts of which it is composed ; the fate of an empire, in many respects, the most interesting in the world." In the second number we read : " It is worthy of remark, that not only the first, but every succeeding Congress, as well as the late Convention, have invariably joined with the people in thinking that the prosperity of America depended on its Union. To preserve and perpetuate it was the great object of the people in forming that Convention ; and it is also the great object of the plan which the Convention has advised them to adopt. . . . They who promote the idea of substituting a number of distinct confederacies in the room of the plan of the Convention, seem clearly to foresee that the rejection of it would put the continuance of the Union in the utmost jeopardy ; that certainly would be the case ; and I sincerely wish that it may be as clearly foreseen by every good citizen, that whenever the dissolution of the Union arrives, America will have reason to exclaim, in the words of the poet :

'FAREWELL ! A LONG FAREWELL TO ALL MY GREATNESS !' "

Having alluded to the *Federalist*, let me add that the statesmanlike pleas of this noble work in behalf of the Union, and its vivid pictures of the perils and woes of disunion, would still form one of the best possible tracts for the times. It seems as if the chapters, "Concerning dangers from war between the States," "The effects of internal war in producing standing armies, and other institutions unfriendly to liberty," "The utility of the Union as a safeguard against domestic faction and insurrection," were written yesterday, rather than seventy years ago, so applicable are they to the present crisis.

The politicians who favored the theory of distinct, independent confederacies — a theory never heard of until engendered amidst the heated and angry disputes consequent upon the Convention of '87—opposed the new Constitution on the express ground that, once adopted, it for ever closed the door against their favorite doctrine. I doubt if the most diligent research among the newspapers, pamphlets, popular addresses, and debates in State conventions during the period in question, would discover a single passage—I do not say by an eminent statesman or publicist, but a single passage by any body, the most obscure partisan—asserting the right of a State, once in the new Union, to leave it at pleasure. No such right was maintained in respect of the existing Union. The only way, I repeat it, in which the advocates of distinct confederacies hoped to carry out their theory, was by letting the old Union, already little better than a wreck, go to pieces; once embarked in the "more perfect Union," which they saw to be staunch, oak-ribbed and well manned, built on purpose to plough the vast sea of time, with *E Pluribus Unum* emblazoned upon its star-spangled banner—once embarked in this strong constitutional Union, they knew full well that the States must sail on together, and share a common destiny.

But even were it true that in forming this more perfect Union, the American people had no distinct intention that it should be perpetual, such appears very plainly to have been the intention of nature and Providence. There's a divinity that shapes the ends of States as of individuals, rough-hew them as they will. The contingent and unconscious forces that impel a nation forward in its predestined path, are hardly less important than those which proceed of deliberate choice and design. Had the authors of the *Federalist* foreseen that in less than half a century it would be easier to send a message from New-York to Portland or Savannah than it then was to send a message from New-York to Hoboken, that a journey from New-York to Philadelphia would be made in less time than was then required to go to a neighboring village; had they foreseen that in less than three quarters of a century time and distance would be virtually annihilated, and the Atlantic and Pacific oceans brought, as it were, within sound of each other's voices, their arguments for the Union and the Constitution, founded upon the configuration of the continent and the designs of Providence, would have possessed to their minds all the force of a mathematical demonstration. The steamboat, the railroad, and the magnetic telegraph have already so reduced the scale of distances, and brought the remotest points of the Union into such neighborly relations, that the whole country is now in reality hardly less compact, and the different parts of its population in hardly less close connection with each other, than was the case with the Empire State and the different portions of its population on the day when Washington was inaugurated as our first President. These mighty instruments of national and social advancement have facilitated the extension and onward march of the Republic, in a manner undreamt of by the most far-sighted among its founders; they have furnished invincible reasons why it should remain for ever one and indivisible, which the boldest prophet of its future greatness would then have pronounced altogether visionary. This is only a specimen of what time, or rather let us say, what Providence, has done to justify the wisdom of our sires. But, in truth, all the capital inventions and improvements, the whole progress of the past eighty years, whether in agriculture, navigation, manufactures, mining, and the mechanic acts; in education, in political and social science, in literature, in public journalism, or in the sphere of religion and Christian philanthropy—all have fallen in with the growth of the Union, adding at once to its power and beneficence.

The American Union, I am aware, has been widely regarded by foreigners, and sometimes at home also, as an exceedingly artificial system; as having no proper centre; and sure, therefore, sooner or later, to break in pieces. It has been supposed to be the product of mere political theory and calculation rather than the natural, organic development of national life. Whether or not this is so, is the momentous question now wavering in the balance. It does not become us to dogmatize too confidently upon a point which the inexorable logic of events is hastening to decide. But for my own part I still hold, with unfaltering conviction, that our Union, as a whole and in all its parts, is in an extraordinary degree the genuine outgrowth of the race and the soil, and that it could not have been materially different from what it is without being in conflict with its own history and vital principles. It was ordained from the beginning to be a free, self-governing, representative republic;—a democratic, Christian commonwealth.

I do not believe there is a state in Christendom, or
2

that there was a state in the ancient world, not excepting Greece and Rome, marked by a more distinct or a more potential and exuberant individual life. Whether we watch it emerging on the Rock of Plymouth to take posses-sion of the continent, or at a later age see it, grown hardy by suffering and toil, rising up to wrest its independence from the strong arm of England, and then reörganizing its institutions and liberties in a new Magna Charta; or follow it, still advancing in its wonderful career, during the past seventy years, it is always and everywhere the same free, progressive, self-reliant, practical and yet ideal power; full of infinite resource and versatility; honoring the past, master of the present, abounding in hope; a power equally at home in field and forest, in work-shop, counting-room or study, on land and ocean, around the fireside and at the altar—conscious of a great mission for the good of man and the glory of God, and resolved to fulfil it, let who and what will oppose.

The finest personal character is one in which the spontaneous and voluntary elements, the fresh, genial impulses of youth and the reflective wisdom of age are most perfectly blended; or, to express it differ-ently, in which intelligent plan shapes and directs, with-out repressing, the warm, vital forces of the soul; for these are, so to say, the capital and reserved fund of all grand characters. Now the state has its peculiar life as well as the individual, and the perfect develop-ment of that life in both is subject to conditions not dissimilar. In the state, too, there should be a harmonious blending of the spontaneous and the de-liberate, wise counsel and choice, inspired by great national sentiments and traditions. I admit that in forming the Constitution of the United States there was a high exercise of political reflection and choice; but it was reflection based upon a profound acquaintance with the history, institutions, and spirit of the country; it was a choice full of purest zeal for the general good, a choice guided by the public reason and actuated by the popular will, a choice and reflection, in fine, which embodied the inmost thought and desire of the whole nation; so that the Constitution is as real a product and exponent of the character and mind of the American people as the treatises on the *Freedom of the Will* and the *Religious Affections* are a true expression of the intellect and piety of the great theologian of New-England, or as *Paradise Lost* is a faithful reflection of the epic genius of Milton. There is a sense, unquestionably, in which our system of government may be fairly described as artificial and complicate. But is not this true of the best things in the world? The higher you rise in the sphere of individual or social life, the more numerous the elements and conditions of excellence, the more numerous the checks and counter-checks, the wheels within wheels. The life of a plant is far simpler than that of a bird; the life of an insect than that of a child; and the life of a child than that of a man. The nobler the life, the more its organs and modes of expression are enriched and multiplied. What an exceedingly artificial and complicate piece of workmanship is the human eye! It seems as if the Divine Artist himself must have paused to reflect and choose before fashioning such a peerless window for admitting and emitting light and beauty! Consider any eminently original and perfect type of character, whether of manhood or saintliness, and I am sure you will find what I have been saying verified to the letter. Such a character is the rare product of varied forces; and it impresses us with admiration, because it has had the will and the skill to combine and shape these varying, oft opposing, forces, reason, understanding, fancy, sentiment, experience, age, country, circumstances, good and ill, into one symmetrical, finished whole, into the living hero, patriot, or sage. Now the free State is, as I have said, the grandest work of man; it is the hiding-place and strength of a nation's life, the *house not made with hands*, in which its successive generations find shelter, protection, and a home, on their way to eternity. It establishes for them justice; insures their domestic tranquillity; provides for their common defence; promotes their general welfare; and secures the blessings of liberty to them and their posterity. What a vast, powerful, and wisely-ordered system it must needs be to execute such a task as this without weariness, from age to age, even as the heavenly bodies move on in their benignant courses! What strong diversities must help to form and buttress this sublime unity! "Every free government"—I quote one of the weightiest sentences of Daniel Webster—"Every free government is necessarily complicated, because all such governments establish restraints as well on the power of government itself as on that of individuals. If we will abolish the distinction of branches, and have but one branch; if we will abolish jury trials, and leave all to the judge; if we will then ordain that the legislator shall himself be the judge; and if we place the executive power in the same hands, we may readily simplify government. We may easily bring it to the simplest of all forms, a pure despotism."

But "the American Union," it is said further, "has no *centre;* and it is impossible now to make one. The more they extend their border into the Indian's land, the weaker will the national cohesion be."* This ob-

---

* Coleridge's *Table Talk*, vol. ii. p. 53. He adds: "But I look upon the States as splendid masses, to be used, by and by, in the composition of

jection seems to me to overlook the peculiar constitution of American society, and the difference between a visible, or formal, centre, and a *central principle;* in other words, the principle of nationality. The latter certainly belongs to the Union in a very high degree; and is not that the strongest bond of "national cohesion"? So far from growing weaker, has it not grown more powerful as we have extended our border into the Indian's land? Are Wisconsin, Iowa, Minnesota, and Kansas, or even California and Oregon, less patriotic than Maine, and New-York, and New-Jersey? Are the Alleghanies or the Rocky Mountains any barrier to the free, centripetal forces of the Republic? The truth is, the centre of our Union is everywhere; it cannot from its very nature be strictly and fully localized; it is, like our self-government, a diffused, omnipresent principle, or, as is said of the soul, it is *all in every part.* And yet, in the ordinary sense of the term, has not the Union quite as much of a centre as Switzerland, one of the oldest and toughest nationalities of Europe? But I have no time to dwell longer upon these points, although they merit a much fuller discussion.

Thus far I have spoken chiefly in terms of praise and

two or three great governments." A few months later he says: "The possible destiny of the United States of America, as a nation of a hundred millions of freemen, stretching from the Atlantic to the Pacific, living under the laws of Alfred, and speaking the language of Shakspeare and Milton, is an august conception. *Why should we not wish to see it realized?* America would then be England viewed through a solar microscope: Great Britain in a state of glorious magnification." What a contrast between this generous catholic spirit and that which, since our troubles began, has breathed in the London *Times, Saturday Review,* and other anti-American organs of English public opinion! The malicious glee with which this most influential section of the British press has calumniated, ridiculed, and mocked at the American people in this day of their calamity, is a disgrace to the civilization and humanity of the age.

honor, as the purpose of my address naturally led me
to do. But I am far, indeed, from thinking that our
political system is perfect even in theory, much less
that it has been so in practice. The best institutions
are liable to be abused even as the very truth of
God may be changed into a lie. Nothing in this world
is perfect; no work of man which is not tainted with
moral evil and does not share in its dread penalties.
The old providential laws are still in full force; and no
government is so well constituted or so strong as to be
able to violate them with impunity. The conditions of
true national prosperity are exceedingly severe, and
they do not change. The divine Nemesis, which exe-
cutes judgment upon the sins of states and nations,
never stops to ask whether they bear the name of de-
mocracy or of monarchy; whether they belong to the
Anglo-Saxon or any other race. *Die Welt-geschichte ist
das Welt-gericht.* It were folly to deny that during the
last quarter of a century—not to go further back—vices
of the worst sort have been preying upon our national
life. The sacred ideas of law, government, and patriotism have suffered a fearful eclipse. A reckless, un-
scrupulous and venal temper has shown itself in every
department of public affairs. The energy of the moral
forces of the State has been altogether inadequate to
restrain or serve as a counterpoise to the high-pressure
activity and excitement of the material forces. The
process of political degeneracy has been rapid and over-
whelming. From standing very high in the estimation
of wise and good men abroad, our country has become the object of wide-spread and growing dislike in
the old world. The revolution of European public
opinion respecting us, since De Tocqueville published
his celebrated work, is something hard to be believed
by any one who has not himself had occasion actually

to witness and feel it. The sins of old, worn-out des-
potisms, it is alleged, have reäppeared, full-blown, in our
young republic. We have developed, it is said, a preco-
city in political vice and corruption, which shows plainly
that we are rotting before we are ripe. That there has
been too much occasion for these grave charges, is indis-
putable. I will not go into details. This is not the
place ; nor would I like to trust myself to say all that
might truly be said on this subject. I will merely
mention, by way of illustration, the huge system of corruption, bribery and swindling connected with the
municipal government of our commercial metropolis and
with the public legislation at Washington, Albany and
elsewhere ; the scandal of repudiation, the rapidly-
increasing sale of votes, the barbarous spoils-system,
with the frenzied greed and scramble for office engendered by it ; the Border-ruffian scenes and elections in
Kansas ; the vulgar and brutal outbreaks in Congress ;
the dearth of eminent statesmen, and the multiplication
of political demagogues ; the wholesale prosecution
of the African slave-trade, under the protection of the
American flag ; fillibusterism, Floydism, and the new
gospel of the divine institution, beneficence and unlimited extension of negro slavery. These are some of
the things which have shaken the faith of foreign nations, and to a certain extent, our own faith, in the
wisdom and perpetuity of our democratic institutions.
They are evils which the founders of the Union neither
foresaw, nor could provide against. They have sprung
in part from that abuse of freedom which nothing but
the highest popular virtue and intelligence can resist,
and partly from causes lying deep in human nature, in
the circumstances of the country and the times ; and in
all exercise of power by selfish, erring mortals. It is
impossible rightly to understand the present crisis with-

out carefully studying them. They have been slowly
and stealthily preparing the mine which has now exploded with such terrific effect. It was in the abominable school of Mississippi repudiation in which he took
his first lessons and made his earliest appearance in public life ; it was in advocating the immoral doctrine that
"one generation can not bind another," that Mr. Jefferson Davis was trained to be the leader of a titanic conspiracy for repudiating the government and constitution of his country, with all the oaths and promises
which bound him to it. It was in cheering on "the
gray-eyed man of destiny," William Walker, and in
splendid dreams of seizing Cuba and Central America,
that other of these Southern leaders learned to think so
lightly of stealing the property and assailing the life
of our Union. What atmosphere but one laden with
the malaria of political sophistry and corruption could
have engendered that wholesale *perjury* on the part of
our public men, especially officers of the national army
and navy, which has appalled Christendom ? To show
what the new-fangled doctrine of slavery and its unlimited extension has done to demoralize the country
and plunge it into this Red sea of trouble, would require
a book instead of a passing sentence. Let us be thankful that the dreadful malady, of which these things are
symptoms, is at last forced out upon the surface, and
that we know now what it is and how to treat it. We
see plainly that it is an evil *ense recidendum ;* no gentler
method will conquer it.

And this brings us to another point in our discussion.

I have shown that the Union was intended by the
people who formed it, and that it seems quite as clearly
intended by nature and Providence to be perpetual.
But the practical question, after all, is : Do the American people now upon the stage, the trustees and usu-

fructuaries of this glorious heritage, intend that it shall be perpetual? Are they resolved and able to execute the will of the generations that have gone before them, to carry out the designs of nature and Providence? or will they prove recreant to the tremendous charge? Life and death are set before them: which will they choose? The history of the world affords few instances in which a great people have been so distinctly summoned to face this awful issue. And a few months ago, it must be confessed, the most hopeful had reason for deep misgiving as to the result. It seemed almost as if the nation were really about to abdicate its imperial sovereignty, to bare its bosom to the assassin's dagger, and so die in shame and despair. A kind of moral asphyxia had seized it; and there it lay, month after month, prostrate, and jeered at by the unnatural men whom it had brought up as children and crowned with its fairest honors; its authority defied, its forts and arsenals seized, its money stolen, its renowned flag trampled in the dust, its credit gone, and all the world echoing to the scornful exclamation: *The great Democratic bubble has burst! The model Republic is no more!* When in the early spring the correspondent of the London *Times* passed through New-York, he found the leading citizens, as he avers, in a state of easy indifference, eating and drinking, marrying and giving in marriage, even as the prophetic word tells us it will be at the coming of the Son of Man to judge the world. But we know very well now that all this was an illusion; the dead calm which precedes the whirlwind.

The nation was certainly perplexed in the extreme; but this perplexity was the effect in part of its unsuspecting, magnanimous temper, and partly of the mental confusion caused by the staggering blows of treason. All perplexity, however, was annihilated by the bombardment of Fort Sumter. As the report of that ruth-less cannonade reverberated through the land, it was as if the trump of God had sounded. The nation started up like a man inspired. Its self-consciousness, too long darkened by the strifes of party and absorption in ma-terial interests, returned again *as the morning, fair as the moon, clear as the sun, and terrible as an army with banners.* The old, ancestral spirit was reënthroned; the selfish passions, delusions and prejudices of years were swept away in an instant, and from that hour to this the loyal American people, being of one heart and one mind, have been marching right onward for the de-fence and salvation of the Republic. The assault upon Fort Sumter was not, of course, the cause, it was only the occasion of this miraculous uprising. During the whole winter the way had been preparing for it. The months of November and December, 1860, and of Jan-uary, February and March, 1861, will not easily pass out of the memory of the American people. They were the Valley Forge of our political history. How like a horrid incubus they pressed upon the popular heart! Our manhood as well as our nationality seemed about to abandon us. We saw the Union going upon the rocks, piloted by a perjured band of wreckers ; we saw them tearing down the old flag and spitting upon it in disdain ; we heard them, as they betook them-selves to the boats, and hastened away to their con-federates, shouting in derision that the gallant ship which our fathers built to sail on for ever, was scuttled past help, and would never again ride the ocean wave ; we saw and heard all this. Yet the world moved on as aforetime ; no sign in the heavens betokened that the avenging thunderbolts were about to descend ; the triumph of mingled treachery and imbecility appeared complete.

What a picture history will give of this period of crime, infamy, and cowardice ! Alas ! for the chief conspirators and their abettors when she shall one day draw them at full length, and set them in ever-lasting colors upon her awful canvas ! Well might they pray to have their names effaced for ever from the memory of the Republic !

The twelfth, thirteenth and fourteenth days of April last seem to lie back many years, and the gloomy months preceding are as the days before the flood. Since November, 1860, the nation has been taught, and has in a measure marked, learned, and inwardly digested great permanent lessons of truth and duty, which, under ordinary circumstances, could hardly have been taught and learned in half a century. How plainly we now see that government is an ordinance of God, founded in eternal justice ; that it is not mere influence, nor moral suasion, nor moral reform ; but sovereign authority, armed with divine sanctions, and the sword of vengeance ; that while light to the obedient, it is like lightning to evil-doers ! How plainly we now see that to prostitute this great institution of God to purposes of political corruption, money-making, and self-aggrandizement, is a kind of sacrilege : it is as if the ordinance of marriage were converted into an instrument of lust and adultery ; we have learnt, too, that solemn oaths, unless vivified by the fear of God, will turn to perjury when the day of trial comes, for which they are recorded in heaven ; we have learnt that the price of liberty is, in very deed, eternal vigilance ; and that the neglect of their civil duties by the cultivated, wealthy, and influential classes of society, whether from the mad pursuit of gain, love of ease, dislike to political noise and strife, religious scruples, or whatever other motive, is a high offence against the state and against heaven. The

American people, in a word, have been taught to see that government is something infinitely deeper and higher than the dogmas and triumph of party, the election of Presidents, and all the outward forms and machinery of political action. Never were they better prepared than now to heed the exhortation of the old Puritan poet and patriot, George Wither:

" Let not your King and Parliament in one,
  Much less apart, mistake themselves for that
Which is most worthy to be thought upon ;
Nor think *they* are, essentially, the State.
Let them not fancy, that the authority
And privileges upon them bestown,
Conferred are to set up a majesty,
A power, or a glory, of their own !
But let them know, 't was for a deeper life,
Which they but represent—
That there's on earth a YET AUGUSTER THING,
Veiled though it be, than Parliament and King."

And while the nation has laid to heart these general lessons of political truth and duty, how fast has it learnt to understand the strange events of the day ! What six months ago was deemed a problem too hard to solve, needs no solution now. What then puzzled the understanding of statesmen, scarce puzzles that of children to-day. Read over the messages, speeches, sermons, and editorials about " coercion," which last winter flooded the land, and it will seem next to impossible that so short a period separates now and then. Never before, perhaps, did a nation make such rapid strides in tearing off the coils of political sophistry, casting aside selfish party issues, and educating itself for the sublime work of its own salvation. No thoughtful person, it seems to me, can regard it otherwise than as a special providence of the Almighty. But yesterday, as it were, the whole country was thrown into a state of nervous agitation, and the ancient Commonwealth

of Virginia aroused to the highest pitch of angry excitement because of a rumor that one of the guns of
Fortress Monroe was pointing *inland!* A great many
guns of Fortress Monroe, as well as elsewhere in and
about the " Old Dominion," are now pointing inland,
and are likely to point that way for a long time, not
according to a vague rumor, but by the solemn order
and determination of the Government and people of
the United States. But yesterday, as it were, *coercion*
had been played with such a cunning and masterly
hand, appealing now to the noblest sentiments of Christian charity and patriotism, now to the natural horror
of war and bloodshed, and then to fear, avarice, personal
ambition, and party prejudice ; clothing itself now in
the plausible dress of State Rights and constitutional
argument, and anon of political expediency—*coercion*,
I say, had at length come to signify to myriads of wise
and loyal citizens something most oppressive, reckless,
and cruel. How many wise and loyal American citizens do you think there *now* are to whom *coercion* has
any other meaning than rightful authority, government,
the Constitution, the Union, and the enforcement of the
laws ? But yesterday, as it were, the heresy of *secession*,
(" a word," as the Nestor of the American Bar, Mr.
Binney, has so happily said, " to drug the consciences of
ignorant men who are averse to treason,") this baleful
heresy, had stolen into the Legislative Halls and Cabinet
Council of the country, squatting at first like a toad, to
drop its poisonous suggestions into the unsuspecting
popular ear, half-seducing the aged Chief Magistrate
himself into its toils, then boldly avowing itself in pre-
sence of the astounded nation, and challenging the Government to coerce or resist it ! What to the American
people is " secession" *now*—now that it has been com-
pelled to throw off all disguise, stand up before the

world in its proper character, and enter upon the execution of its long-laid plans? It is what Satan appeared at the touch of Ithuriel's spear—a lying fiend and rebel, a most crafty conspirator against sleeping innocence, against the hopes of humanity, and the righteous order of the world; a spirit of ambitious hate and disobedience, that "would rather reign in hell than serve in heaven." They regard secession, in a word, as a gigantic crime, without a parallel on this continent, and with few parallels in the history of the world; a crime second only to that which should attempt to subvert the divine government itself. It is a crime against our canonized forefathers. It is a crime against the living nation. It is a crime greater still against unborn generations, and against the human race. Such is the opinion which the American people now hold of secession. They regard it as a deadly heresy in point of law, and as wicked treason and rebellion in point of fact. They believe that unless it is put down, both the constitution and the nation must perish; that unless they conquer it, it will conquer and ruin them. In this faith there is little difference between the learned and the plain people; between farmers, merchants, mechanics, professional men and politicians; between native and foreign-born citizens; between Roman Catholics and Protestants. In this faith some two hundred thousand of them, without respect of party, nativity, or religion, have willingly offered their lives to their country, and are already marshaled into the great army of the Union; and hundreds of thousands more are ready to do the same. They look with horror upon the fruits secession has already borne, the crimes it has committed, the reign of terror it has instituted, and the merciless hypocrisy and falsehood by which it has deceived and precipitated into utter anarchy and woe millions of the people. They contemplate with still deeper horror the prospect of its becoming, as it must and will if suffered to live, a consolidated military despotism, based upon negro slavery as its corner-stone, actuated by a contemptuous hatred of free labor and free society, by boundless ambition and lust of territorial aggrandisement, and thus establishing itself as a foreign nation from the shores of the Chesapeake across the continent, holding the Gulf of Mexico and the mouth of the Mississippi, and dictating law to Cuba, Mexico, and Central America. They would deem the abandonment of this immense territory to Spain or Austria a lesser calamity and peril. Hence it is, they have made up their mind, with the blessing of Almighty God, to put down this rebellion, liberate the loyal citizens of the South from its iron despotism, plant again the Stars and Stripes over every fort and city from the Chesapeake to the Rio Grande, or sacrifice their all in the attempt ; and this they have resolved to do, not in malice, not in revenge, not in wrath, but in defence of republican freedom, and as a solemn duty to themselves and their posterity. And never surely did the fires of patriotic devotion burn with a purer or more intense flame in the palmiest days of Greece or Rome, of Italy, Holland, England, or any other land rendered classic by struggles for freedom and national existence. The sentiment which glowed with such fervor in the heart of the pious Israelite finds a faithful echo to-day in the hearts of millions of the American people : *If I for-get thee, O Jerusalem ! let my right hand forget its cunning ; if I do not remember thee, let my tongue cleave to the roof of my mouth, if I prefer not Jerusalem above my chief joy.* They regard it as a sacred debt which they owe to the past and the future — a debt of gratitude to their honored forefathers, and a debt of service to their posterity — to save this free, Christian Republic from the destruction which threatens it. They form the mystic bridge across which, if at all, its untold treasures, accumulated by the toil, the blood, and the wisdom of many ages, must be conveyed to enrich and bless the generations yet unborn. For it is a radical mistake to fancy that the life-and-death struggle, in which we are now engaged, involves our *political* institutions merely; it involves not less our domestic, social, and religious institutions. These are so vitally bound up with those, that it is not possible to separate them; you might as well attempt to separate the heart or brain from the flesh and bones of the natural body; each is essential to the other; each is animated by the same inspired breath of freedom; each rests upon the strong foundation of general law and order; all together form our great Christian state, our national commonwealth. It is American civilization itself, then, that is at stake. To me, at least, it seems as certain as the course of nature, that the nefarious heresy and rebellion which has plunged us already into such an abyss of trouble, would, if successful, utterly demoralize the spirit and character of the American people. It would be a blow to their Christian virtue and manhood so staggering that a century could scarce enable them to recover from it. It would infuse a fatal poison into their moral life-blood. Religion and learning, as well as freedom and humanity, would never cease to weep over their fall. It is not only a question whether at the bidding of a band of detestable conspirators the American people shall divide their ancient inheritance and break in pieces the substantial unity of the nation; it is also and especially the question whether, directly or indirectly, they shall stamp with their approval a doctrine and a crime, which laughs to scorn the sanctity of oaths, turns to mockery the obligations of covenanted faith, and places the existence of society itself at the mercy of disappointed politicians and ambitious, profligate demagogues. Under certain circumstances, at the entreaty of one of your children, you might reluctantly consent to a division of your estate, which yet you regarded as fraught with much evil to all concerned; but would you do so, could you do so without utter shame and self-debasement, under the pressure of a threat that if you did not, your parental authority should be set at naught, the old homestead burnt to ashes, your other children defrauded of their rights, and the desired portion taken by force? After an arrangement based upon such terms, what would be likely to become of your domestic government? How much dignity, order, and peace; how much filial reverence, would henceforth mark your family life? It seems to me, I repeat it, that the contest which has been so ruthlessly forced upon us, is as truly for our social and religious, as for our political blessings. There is not a single one of the great chartered rights and privileges, purchased for us by the toil and sacrifices of the immortal dead, which is not imperiled by this rebellion. This may not appear on the surface; but penetrate to the heart of the matter and you will find that it is even so, nothing more, nothing else. Every nerve and fibre of American life is bound up with the life of the Union. The national government, viewed in the most formal and abstract way, is yet like the shell of the tortoise, which shelters, guards, and conserves the whole organism within. What would become of the living creature were this protective covering crushed and torn off? And what would become of the vital organism of American society, with its thousand tender and sacred offices, if no longer sheltered and shielded

3

by the Constitution and the laws, it were exposed to the assaults of the rude anarchic elements? Let us not delude ourselves. The peril which 'besets us is a peril to all that we hold most dear. Whether this free, Christian country, in whose earth sleeps the dust of so many wise and good men; whose air has been vocal, from the landing of the Pilgrims until now, with the prayers and praises of innumerable saints; whose history has been so full of providence and so prophetic of a grand, benignant future; which has already sent out its boughs unto the sea and its branches unto the river;— whether it is to be handed down to coming generations mutilated and dishonored, a mere fragment of its former self, so that all the world shall mock at it, or, in unshorn strength and beauty, a still mightier organ of human happiness and the glory of God; *this* is the momentous point now to be decided, and for whose decision the hosts of the republic have gathered themselves to battle.

I do not for an instant forget that war, above all, such a war as this, is an unspeakable calamity. It is enough to shake the stoutest heart to look it in the face. There are thousands of families in the farthest North and East, still more in the Middle and Western Free States, which are connected by innumerable tender ties of blood and affection with every part of the South; while in the States of Maryland, Virginia, Kentucky, and Missouri, not to mention others, the effect of the war has been, in the fearful language of Scripture, to *set a man at variance against his father, and the daughter against her mother, and the daughter-in-law against her mother-in-law. And a man's foes are they of his own household.* It is a horrible thing; and every good man must pray fervently that the days of this distress may be shortened, but shortened by the

speedy triumph of the righteous cause and the restitu-
tion of national authority throughout the length and
breadth of the land. Be this grand consummation,
however, near or far off, be the path which leads to it
through a narrow or a wide sea of trouble, the blessing will still be worth a hundredfold more than it will
cost. Has it not been so in all our history and in the
history of the race? When was the vindication and
triumph of a great principle unattended by heavy sacrifices? When did Christian society make a large ad-
vance without first vanquishing a host of enemies?
Think what it cost our fathers to fight through the
long war of independence; how much precious blood,
how much personal and domestic suffering, what losses,
what disappointments! But then think what plentiful
harvests of public and private blessing their children
and children's children have been reaping from those
bitter seeds all these threescore years and ten! Remember that we do not enjoy to-day a solitary civil
or religious privilege which is not perfumed with the
heroic and suffering virtues of former times; not one
which did not cost blood, treasure, and painful toil;
not one which would ever have been ours had not our
patriotic and godly ancestors lived not for themselves
but for their posterity. It was not for themselves, it
was for their children chiefly, that the Pilgrim Fathers
and mothers became exiles in Holland, and then
crossed the ocean to lay the foundation of an ampler
order of humanity upon the desolate shores and in the
savage wilderness of the new world. It was for us
rather than themselves that the adventurous and brave
settlers of Virginia and New-York laid the foundations
of commercial and political empire. It was, in a word,
for their children rather than themselves that all our
fathers, of whatever name or nation, felled the aboriginal

forests, drove out the heathen before them, and sowed broadcast over the continent the prolific seeds of Law, Religion, Freedom, Intelligence, domestic Joy, and virtuous Industry. It was for us that Washington, and all his sage and valiant compatriots, labored, struggled, thought and spoke. And what eminently wise and good men, in Church and State, have ever since been working on in the self-same spirit, still spending and being spent for our sakes and not their own! And now in turn the solemn task is devolved upon us. •We are summoned by Divine Providence to see to it that, in spite of all opposition, the immortal work still goes forward. The task, I admit, is formidable beyond expression. Our fathers never encountered such a pitiless storm of sedition and treason as now beats upon us; none of them ever faced a moment so big with issues, good or bad for the human race. If our Washington himself, leaving for a while his eternal rest, should come back to be our Leader, and if the most renowned statesmen of his and later times, Hamilton, Jefferson, John Jay, Madison, Franklin, Pinckney, Marshall, Andrew Jackson, Henry Clay, and the Defender of the Constitution, were to be his counsellors, their combined wisdom, unaided by *the wisdom that is from above*, would not rise to the height of our troubles. Nothing, nothing but the guiding hand and inspiration of Almighty Providence can carry us triumphantly through this crisis. Assuming, as we fairly may, that our armies, under their aged and their youthful chieftains, the illustrious Scott (God bless him!) and the gifted McClellan, will wipe out the memory of the recent defeat and be crowned with complete victory; assuming that their career is to be marked henceforth by all the discipline, valor, and humanity which we desire to see adorning our citizen-soldiery, still, what consum-

mate prudence and good sense, what honest tact, what
magnanimity, what fairness and equity, in a word, what
thoroughly statesmanlike and Christian wisdom will be
required to readjust and settle the affairs of the nation
in the right way! Not less than that which brought
order out of the chaos that preceded the first inaugura-
tion of Washington. But the very magnitude of the
task should stimulate us to tenfold zeal and effort so to
perform it that our work shall be forever memorable
and resplendent in the history of eminent, faithful service done to God and man. It is a truly Apocalyptic
contest, and we may well believe that heaven as well as
earth is looking on with eager eye. What the issue
shall be, we know not; it is in the hands of God; but
the interests involved are so momentous, and the con-
tending forces so gigantic, that the issue, be it what it
may, must needs travel far and wide over the world
and far down the track of time. It is an epochal period; the very days and hours seem to fly past freighted
with historic import. Beyond a doubt, it is a chief
turning-point in our destiny as a people; but whether
the turning-point of destruction or of a new creation,
we cannot tell. And yet, even at such a time as this,
it is a primal duty to hope—especially, to hope in Him
before whom all nations are as nothing. For one I believe we shall live and not die. I believe these agonies
through which we are passing, are not of dissolution,
but the birth-throes of a renovated and higher life. I
can never think that He, who led our fathers like a
flock, is going to abandon us in this perilous hour. He
has a thousand times more interest in this land than
we have. He has been here from the beginning. He
will be here, with His church, long after we are dead.
What hands but His reared this vast asylum and city
of refuge for the poor and oppressed millions of the

old continent? What wisdom but His planned and planted here, midway between Asia and Europe, this growing Temple of Freedom and Humanity, this Pharos to all benighted and tempest-tost nations? And will He now look on and see mad, rebellious hands raze it to the ground? I cannot believe it. I cannot think He is going to destroy a country, which, however griev- ous may have been its faults and follies, was neverthe- less cradled in Christian faith, and is still the home of millions of men, women, and children, whose constant prayer is, that in all its parts, North and South, East and West, and among all classes of its population, black or white, bond and free, His blessed kingdom may come and His will be done as it is done in heaven.

Let us not, then, despair of the Republic. Let us abide steadfast in the faith that it will outride the pre- sent as it has outridden all lesser storms, and that, pu- rified and ennobled by adversity, " casting far from it the rags of its former vices," and inspired more and more by the divine principles in which it was founded, it shall approximate ever nearer to the perfect ideal of a Free, Christian State, and armed with

> Sovereign Law, that State's collective will,
> O'er thrones and globes elate
> Sit Empress, crowning good, repressing ill.

The Free Christian State and the Present Struggle.

AN ADDRESS

DELIVERED BEFORE THE

ASSOCIATION

OF THE

ALUMNI OF BOWDOIN COLLEGE,

BY

GEORGE L. PRENTISS,

AUGUST 8, 1861.

NEW-YORK:

JOHN A. GRAY, PRINTER, STEREOTYPER, AND BINDER.

FIRE-PROOF BUILDINGS,

CORNER OF FRANKFORT AND JACOB STREETS.

1861.